The Little

Red Tail is a mermaid.

1

She lives at the bottom of the sea
with her family and friends.

her mother

Queen Golden Hair

Pink Tail

Green Tail

Here is Red Tail's family.

her father

King White Beard

her sisters

Yellow Tail

Blue Tail

Red Tail has a dream:
"I would like to live on the land.
I would like to have legs to walk,
run and dance."

One day she sees a ship.
There is a boy on the ship.
He's a prince.
"He's very handsome!"
Red Tail thinks.

Suddenly... there is a storm.
The ship sinks and the prince
falls into the sea.

wind

ship

sea

Red Tail swims towards the prince.
She wants to save him.

- clouds
- lightening
- rain
- wave

Red Tail takes the prince to the beach.
But when the prince opens his eyes
Red Tail dives into the sea.
Sea people can't talk to land people.

Red Tail is sad.
"I would like to have legs
and live on the land with the prince."
"Forget the prince," her fish friends say.
But Red Tail thinks, "Maybe the Witch
of the Sea can help me!"

The Witch of the Sea lives in a black cave.
"Witch of the Sea, please give me legs,"
says Red Tail.

seahorse

starfish

shark

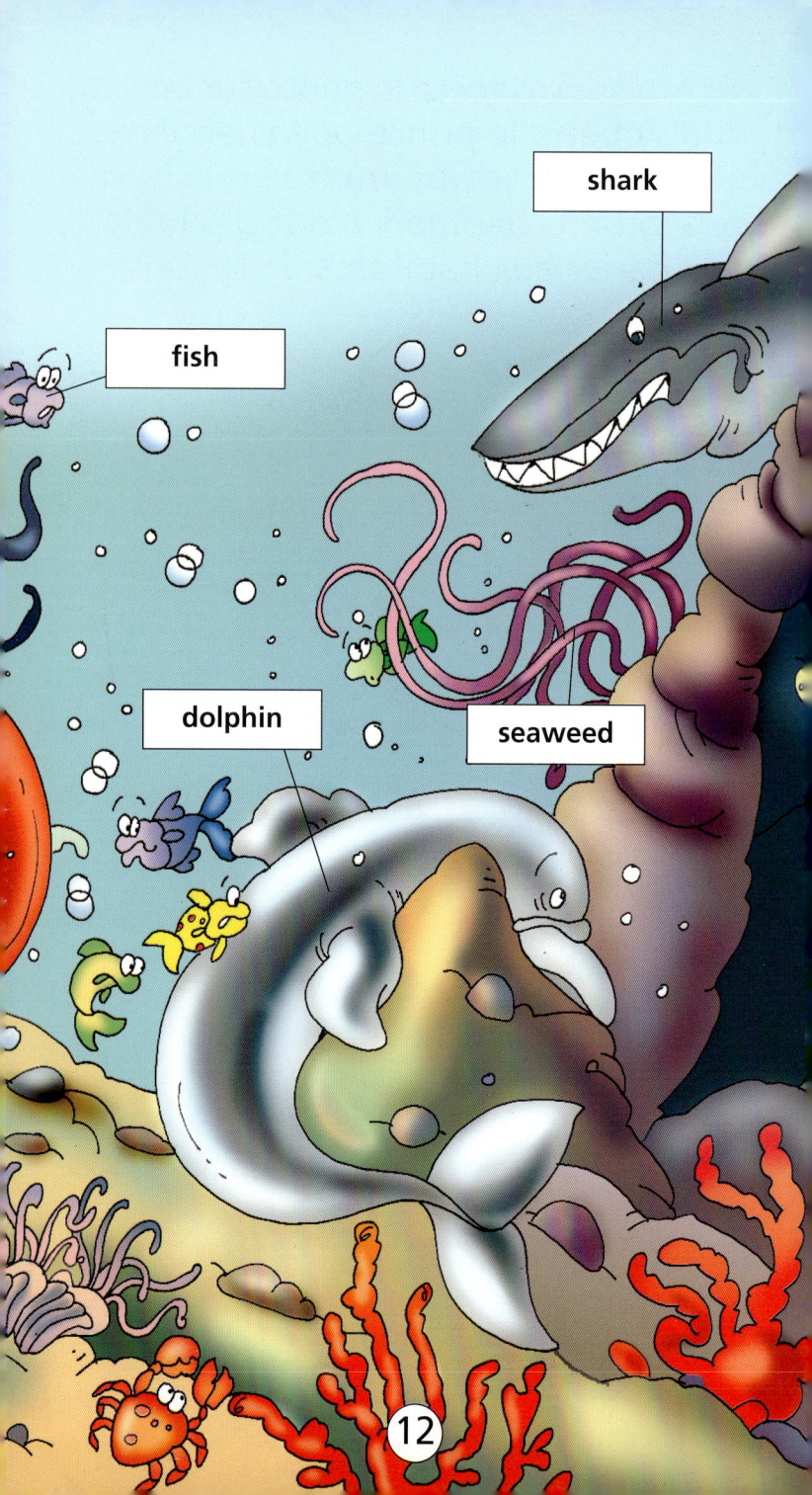

fish

dolphin

seaweed

rock

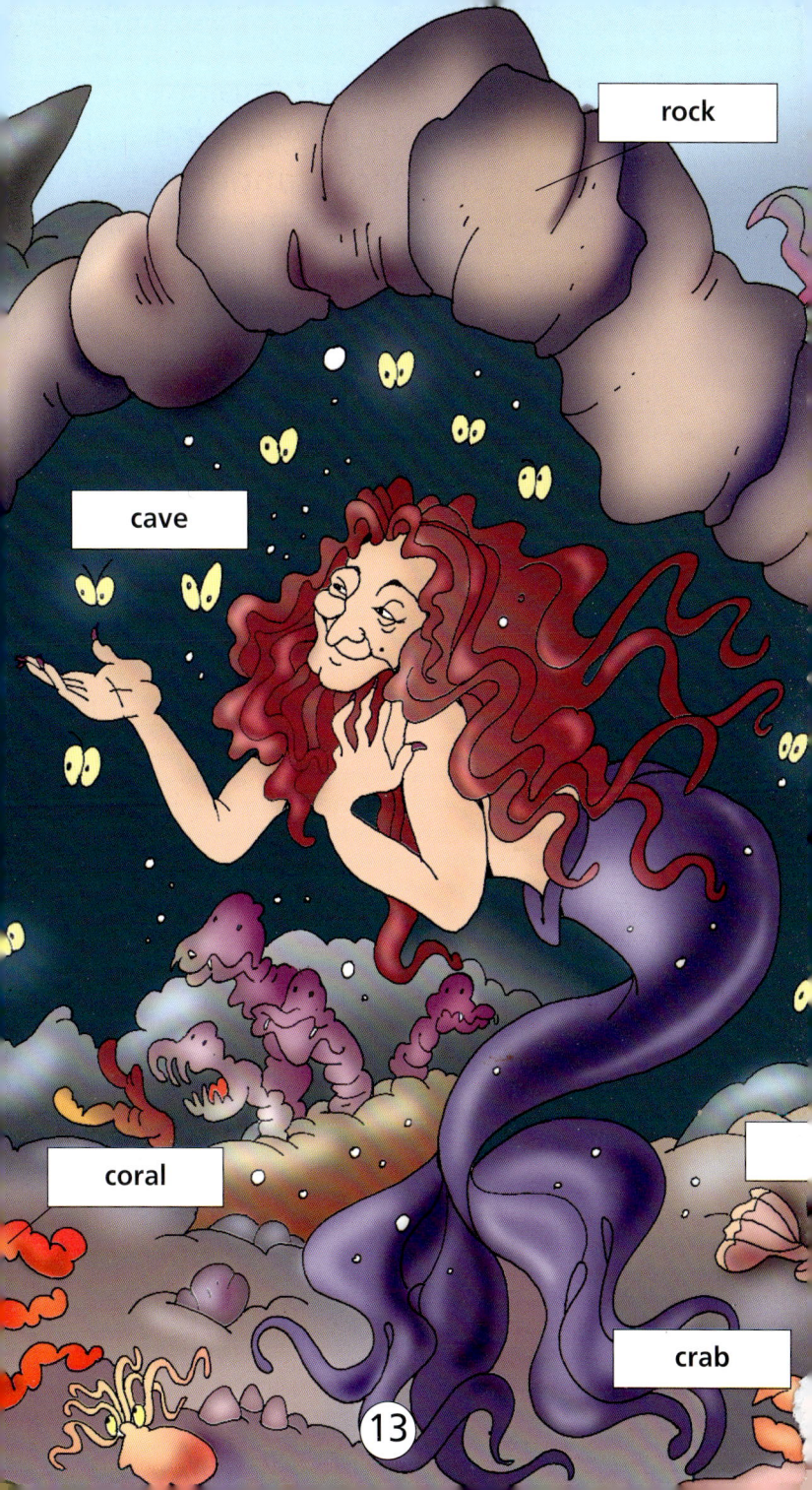

cave

coral

crab

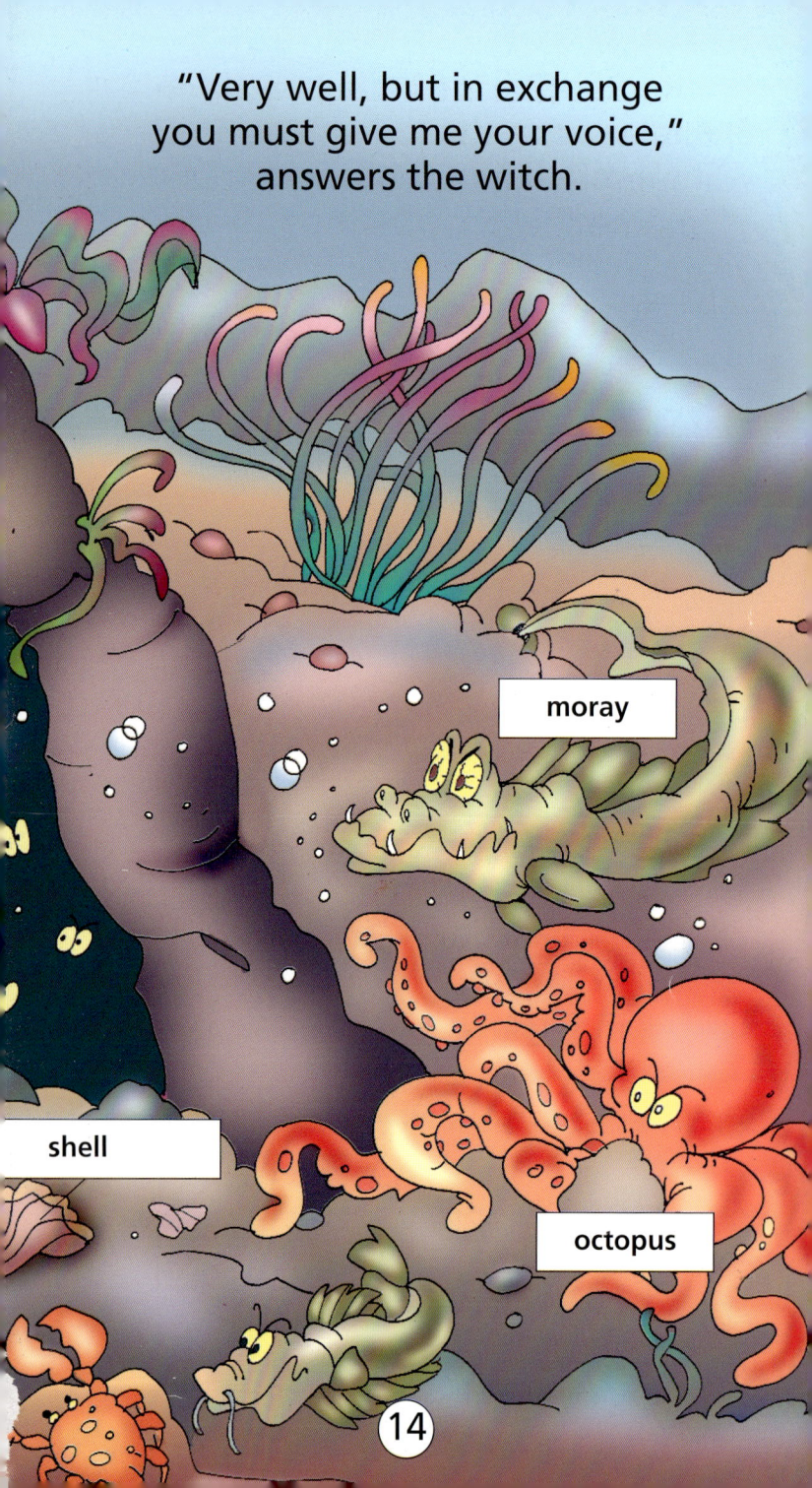

"Very well, but in exchange you must give me your voice," answers the witch.

moray

shell

octopus

Red Tail is on the beach.
She hasn't got a tail, she's got two legs.
She's very happy, but she can't talk.

The prince is on the beach too.
He smiles at Red Tail and asks,
"Hello, what's your name?"
But Red Tail can't answer,
the witch has got her voice.

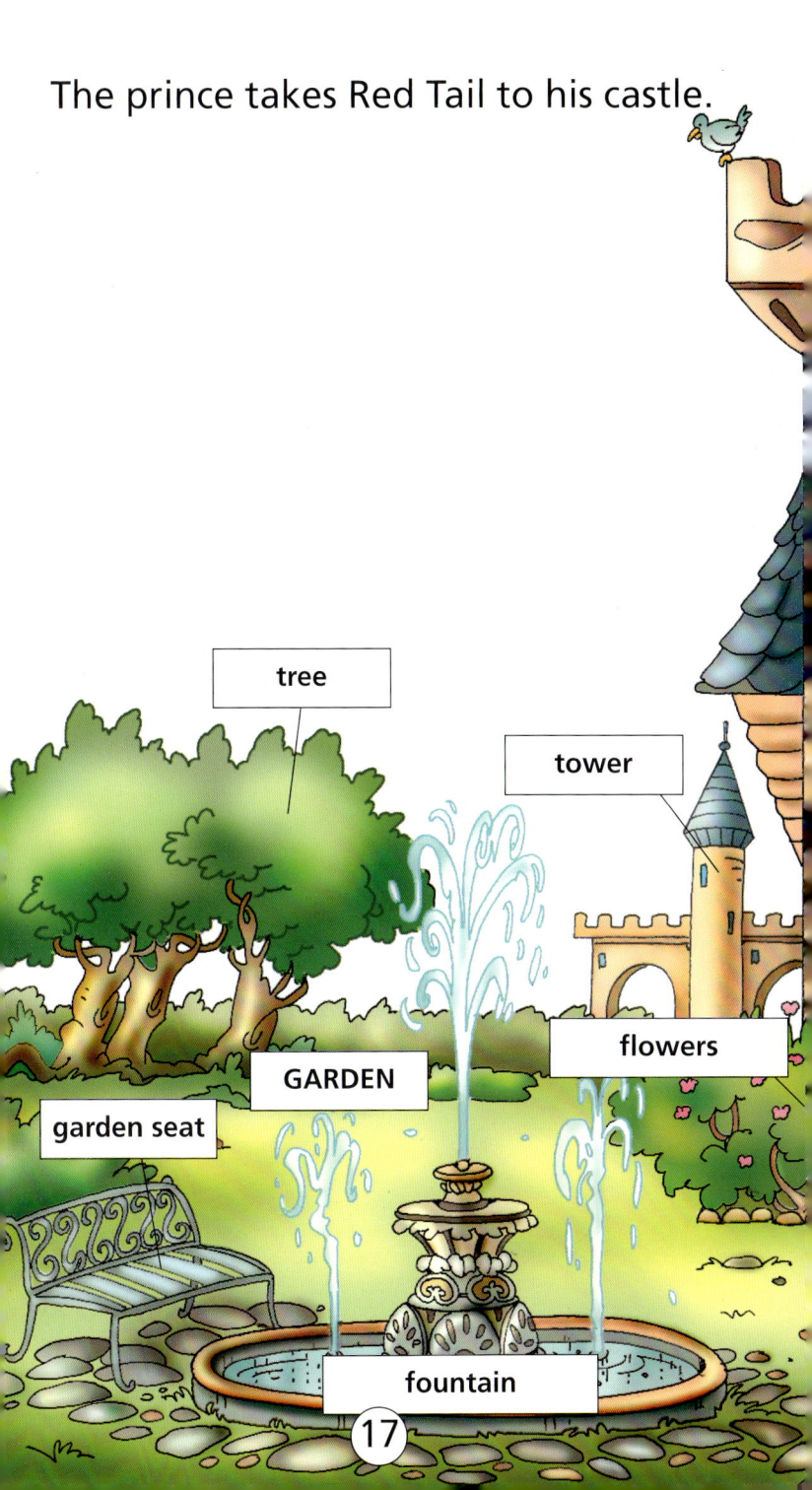

The prince takes Red Tail to his castle.

tree

tower

flowers

GARDEN

garden seat

fountain

window

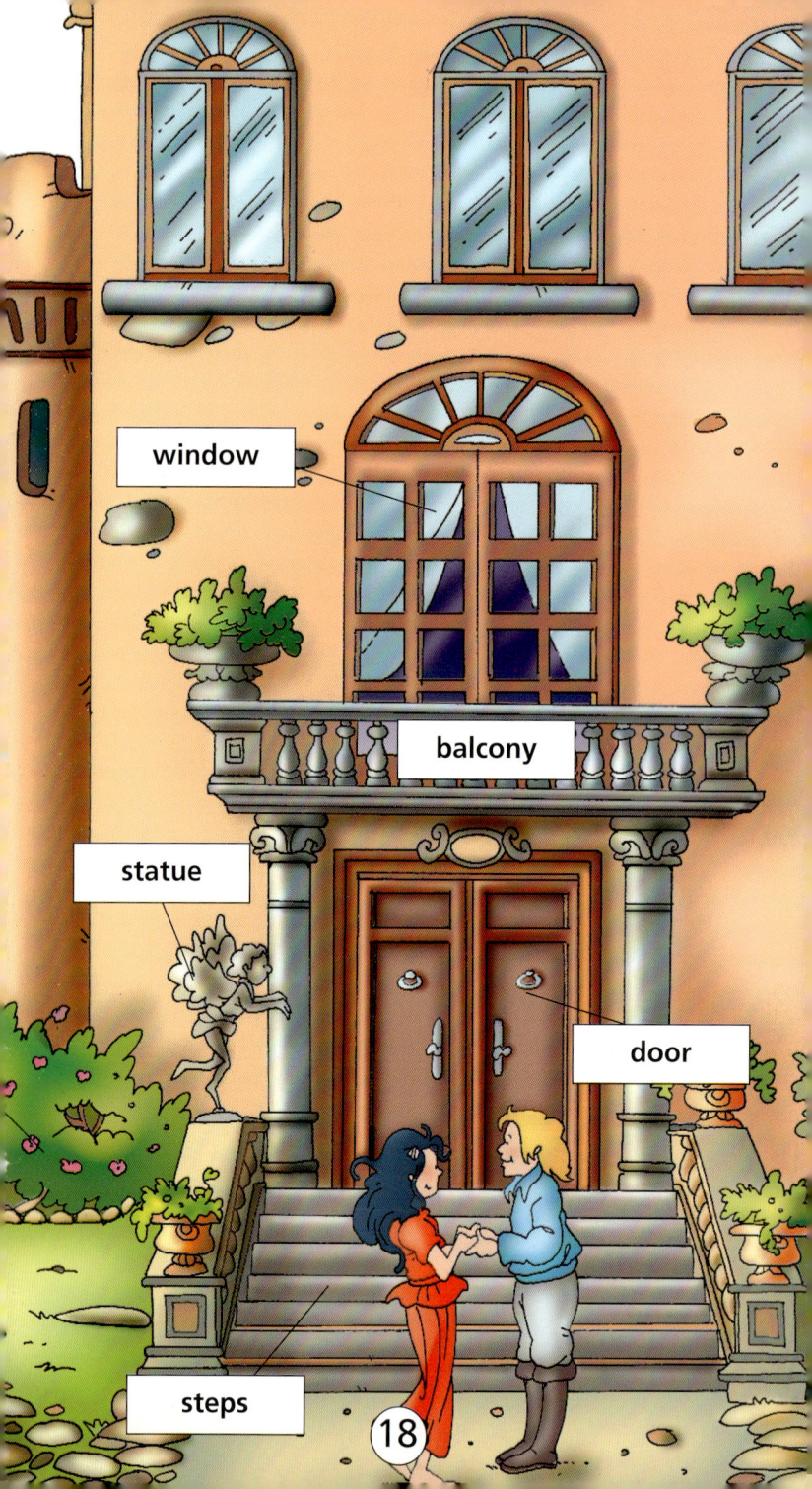

balcony

statue

door

steps

Red Tail is in the castle. She can see the sea from the window of her room. Her friends are jumping and swimming in the waves. Red Tail watches them. She would like to swim with them.

Red Tail is a mermaid again.
She is playing in the sea with her friends. Sometimes she looks at the castle, but she isn't sad.
She prefers being a mermaid and living at the bottom of the sea.

Read and colour

What is in the picture?

1. green
2. pink
3. orange
4. red
5. yellow
6. blue

What is the prince's name?

Find six colours in the word search and then read the other letters.

G	R	E	E	N	E	P
R	B	L	U	E	C	I
O	R	A	N	G	E	N
I	R	E	D	V	A	K
Y	E	L	L	O	W	L

The prince's name is P L C E V A L S

Crossword

1. MORAY
2. DULFIN
3. STARFAISH
4. SEAHAH
5. SHARB (SHARK)
6. CRAB
7. FISH
8. OCTOPUS
9. SSELB

Find the differences.

the differences ar 1) the dolphin
2) the Brens 3. the thert claw 4) the
third sail 5, te color of the way

True or false

		V	F
1.	Red Tail is a dolphin.	☐	☒
2.	Red Tail has got four sisters.	☒	☐
3.	Red Tail's father has got a white beard.	☒	☐
4.	Red Tail wants to live on the land.	☒	☐
5.	The Witch of the Sea wants Red Tail's hair.	☐	☒
6.	The prince lives in a castle.	☒	☐

© 1999 - **ELI** s.r.l.
P.O. Box 6 - Recanati - Italy
Tel. +39 071 750701 - Fax +39 071 977851 - www.elionline.com

Illustrated by Elena Staiano

All rights reserved. No part of this publication may be reproduced in any form or by any means or for any purpose without the prior permission of ELI.

Printed in Italy - Tecnostampa - Recanati 07.83.304.0
ISBN 9788881483600